sustainable TRANSPORTATION

**HOW CAN WE
SAVE OUR
WORLD?**

sustainable
TRANSPORTATION

Cath Senker

ARCTURUS

This edition first published by Arcturus Publishing
Distributed by Black Rabbit Books
123 South Broad Street
Mankato
Minnesota MN 56001

Copyright © 2009 Arcturus Publishing Limited

Printed in the United States

Series concept: Alex Woolf
Editor and picture researcher: Patience Coster
Designer: Phipps Design
Consultant: Professor Roger Kemp, Lancaster University, UK

Library of Congress Cataloging-in-Publication Data

Senker, Cath.
  Sustainable transportation / Cath Senker.
      p. cm. -- (How Can We Save Our World?)
  Includes index.
  ISBN 978-1-84837-287-0 (hardcover)
  1. Transportation--Juvenile literature. I. Title.

  HE152.S766 2010
  388--dc22
                              2009000622

Picture Credits
Corbis: 9, 10 (Hulton-Deutsch Collection), 13 (Alessia
Pierdomenico/epa), 15 (Adnan Abidi/Reuters), 19 (Mario
Anzuoni/Reuters), 32 (Bo Zaunders), 35 (Yossan), 41 (Oliver Strewe),
42 (Ashley Cooper), 43 (Susanne Dittrich/zefa); EASI-Images: 11
(Ed Parker), 18 (Adrian Cooper), 25 (Rob Bowden), 26 (Rob Bowden),
31 (Chris Fairclough), 33 (Rob Bowden), 37 (Rob Bowden), 39 (Roy
Maconachie); Getty Images: 22 (H. John Maier Jr./Time Life Pictures);
Science Photo Library: 38 (Patrick Dumas/EURELOIS); Shutterstock:
cover (Johannes Compaan), 6 (Glen Jones), 7 (Gregory Pelt),
8 (IgorXIII), 17 (INNOCENt), 20 (Jim Parkin), 21 (egd), 23
(Jan Kranendonk), 27 (Losevsky Pavel), 28 (Adrian Linley), 29
(Elena Yakusheva); TopFoto: 14 (ImageWorks), 36 (Ray Roberts)

CONTENTS

Transportation and the Climate Crisis

We travel for many reasons: to go to work or school, for business, or to visit friends. We rely on transportation to move goods to where they are needed. A well-functioning transportation system is essential for a country's economy.

Most of the transportation we use depends on fossil fuels: coal, gas, and oil. Yet these sources are not sustainable. There is a limited amount of them, and at some point they will run out. Also, the cost of extracting them is likely to rise dramatically. Oil companies have already pumped out the oil that is relatively easy to access. As time goes on, they will have to pump out oil that is harder to reach. This will cost more money.

There is a similar problem with natural gas. In areas where demand is highest, for example, North America, Europe, and China, supplies are rapidly being used up. Such areas will need to import gas, and this will be costly. The world's supplies of coal are running out too. But a shortage of fossil fuels is not the only problem; their use is causing climate change. In terms of the environment, it is not sustainable to continue burning fossil fuels.

This student relies on bus transportation to get her to school every day.

Climate change

Earth is surrounded by layers of gases, including water vapor, carbon dioxide (CO_2), methane, and nitrous oxide. These are known as "greenhouse gases".

These gases prevent some of the heat from escaping and keep the earth at the right temperature for life to continue. Over the past hundred years, emissions of carbon dioxide, methane, and nitrous oxide by industry, agriculture, and transportation have greatly increased. There is now an excess of greenhouse gases in the earth's atmosphere. The trapped heat has led to a warming of the earth and changes in the climate.

When fossil fuels are used to power transportation, they emit large quantities of greenhouse gases, especially carbon dioxide. Transportation accounts for 14 percent of global greenhouse gas emissions. It is the third-largest source of emissions, jointly with agriculture and industry. We have to think about how to make different forms of transportation more sustainable. We also need to consider how to cut down our requirements for transportion, for example, by using more locally sourced goods and even reducing the amount we travel.

One effect of climate change has been more frequent hurricanes. Hurricane Katrina hit the city of New Orleans in 2005.

FACE THE **FACTS**

The chart below compares average CO_2 emissions from rail, car, and air travel in the United Kingdom (UK).

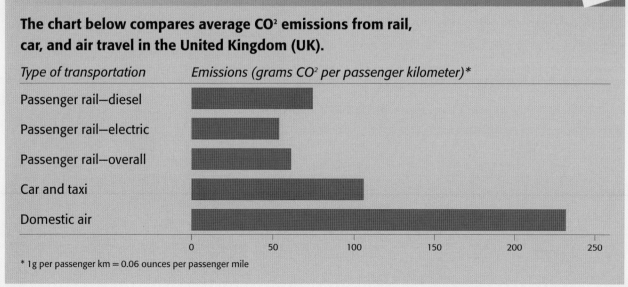

Type of transportation	Emissions (grams CO_2 per passenger kilometer)*

* 1g per passenger km = 0.06 ounces per passenger mile

Source: Association of Train Operating Companies, UK, 2007

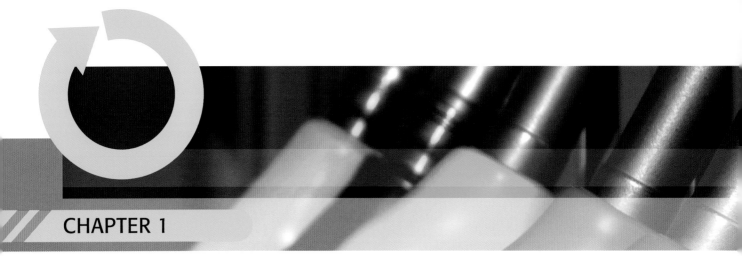

CHAPTER 1

From Animal Power to Aircraft: The History of Transportation

Throughout history, people have used human or animal power to travel. They have walked, ridden camels or horses, or sailed boats. In some parts of the world, these forms of transportation are still in everyday use. About 300 years ago, other forms of transportation began to be developed that relied on fuel to work.

This barge carries sand on the Vistula River in Poland. A barge can transport a huge quantity of bulky cargo.

In Britain, in the eighteenth century, a revolution in transportation took place. People needed a means of moving bulky materials such as coal, iron ore, and limestone from the mines to the new centers of industry. A system of canals was therefore constructed across Britain. Goods were transported along the canals in barges. At the same time, roads were greatly improved so that coaches could travel more quickly and cheaply. However, barges and coaches still relied on horses to pull them.

Railroads

In the early nineteenth century, the steam engine was invented, powered by burning coal. In the 1820s, George Stephenson built the Rocket, the first steam locomotive. He opened the first passenger railroad in

1830, between Liverpool and Manchester. Railroad building proceeded rapidly in Britain and other countries, as did the Industrial Revolution.

Streetcars

As large numbers of people moved to the new industrial centers to work, demand increased for transportation in urban areas. In the late nineteenth century, the use of electric power was developed. Coal was burned in power stations to produce electricity, which was carried along power lines to where it was needed. Electricity was used to power streetcars. Streetcars run on fixed tracks set into the road. Each streetcar draws current from an overhead wire that supplies electric power.

Underground railroads

During the nineteenth century, the huge increase in passenger numbers led to the building of underground railroads beneath major cities such as London, Paris, and New York. Like trains aboveground, the underground trains were steam driven.

FACE THE **FACTS**

The chart below shows the rapid growth of the railroad system in nineteenth-century Europe.

| | Length of line open, in miles * | | |
	1840	1880	1900
Austria-Hungary	89	11,500	22,574
Belgium	207	2,555	2,853
France	308	14,346	23,680
Germany	290	21,025	32,111
Great Britain	1,485	15,571	18,690
Italy	12	5,772	10,208
Netherlands	11	1,147	1,725
Russia	17	14,207	33,078
Spain	–	4,654	8,210
Sweden	–	3,651	7,023

* 1 mile = 1.6 km

Source: *Modern History Sourcebook, Spread of Railways in the 19th Century*

In New York in 1900, roads were dug up in order to build an underground railroad. The New York subway opened in 1904.

This London chauffeur drives an early Daimler car in 1906, before the days of mass-produced vehicles.

Cars

In the late nineteenth century, the invention of the private automobile led to a further revolution in transportation. After various efforts to build cars powered by steam or electricity, it was the development of the internal combustion engine—fueled by gasoline—that provided the key to success.

Car production expanded in Europe and the United States. At first, a car was a luxury item that only the super-rich could afford. In the early years of the twentieth century, Henry Ford of the Ford Motor Company in the US decided to produce cheap, easy-to-run cars. Companies in other countries followed suit. By 2002, there were 590 million cars in the world, most of them in developed countries.

Air travel

In 1903, American brothers Wilbur and Orville Wright made the first engine-powered flight in a biplane—a double-winged airplane. From then on, the aviation industry grew. During World War II (1939-45), aircraft technology improved significantly, and aircraft became larger and faster. After the war, air travel expanded massively. In 2007, the world's airlines recorded 29.7 million flights—an average of 80,987 takeoffs every day.

Unequal access

The developments in transportation have been remarkable, but they have spread unevenly across the world. In developed countries, there are many transportation options, but large numbers of people in developing countries lack sufficient transportation. Women may walk long distances every day to find food and water, while children cover several miles on foot to go to school. In both rich and poor countries, the poorest don't have the transportation they need while the richest people can drive or fly whenever they like. The question is: How can transportation be provided to everyone and yet be made more sustainable?

These children in Congo, eastern Africa, have no access to transportation. They use a wheelbarrow to carry goods.

PERSPECTIVE

Transportation for all

"Almost everywhere, transport priorities serve the poor badly and devote most investment to the mobility of affluent [rich] vehicle owners. The negative impacts of transport fall most heavily on disadvantaged people—those living in poverty, people with disabilities, women, the young, the frail elderly, and people with insecure housing rights. Social equity [fairness] demands that highest priority should go to public transport, walking, and non-motorized vehicles that are accessible to almost everyone and that have low impacts [on the environment]."

Paul Barter and Tamim Raad in *Taking Steps: A Community Action Guide to People-Centred, Equitable and Sustainable Transport*, 2000.

CHAPTER 2

Up in the Skies

Air transportation allows passengers to travel long distances that could not be covered easily by other methods. It means people can travel short distances much more quickly than they could by train or car. Air freight is also the swiftest way for businesses to deliver goods to their destination.

In 2007, the International Air Transport Association predicted that the number of air passengers would rise by 620 million between 2006 and 2011 to a total of 2.8 billion. Air freight would increase by 24 percent during the same period. Why is this increase in air transportation a problem?

High-altitude emissions

All aircraft emit carbon dioxide and other gases. Flying produces roughly the same amount of carbon dioxide per passenger mile as driving. However, when people fly, they can cover great distances. Also, the gases emitted by aircraft have a particularly damaging effect at high altitude. According to the Intergovernmental Panel on Climate Change, the warming effect of aircraft

PERSPECTIVE ●

Airport expansion must stop!

In 2008, two activists from the environmental group Plane Stupid climbed onto the roof of the Scottish Parliament to protest against the expansion of Scottish airports. One of the protesters, Andrew Weymouth, said: "We are facing a runaway climate threat, but the Scottish government's reaction is to triple air traffic and expand Glasgow and Edinburgh airports... The climate scientists have made it clear—we have to stop airport expansion."

emissions is about double that of carbon dioxide alone. So a return flight from London to New York has a similar effect on the climate as driving an average car for a whole year. Transporting freight by air uses huge amounts of fuel too. Flying two pounds (about 1 kilogram) of asparagus from California to the UK uses 900 times more energy than growing it locally!

Traffic in the skies

While aircraft emissions are bad for the environment, there are other problems connected with air transportation. The skies above busy airports are full of aircraft. For example, during rush hours, many planes stack up in the sky over airports in the New York region, waiting for a landing slot. This congestion affects people living nearby, who experience noise pollution from planes circling overhead as well as from planes landing and taking off. Airports also occupy valuable land. In 2008, plans to build a second runway at Stansted Airport in the UK involved the destruction of almost 2,000 acres (800 hectares) of countryside.

In 2008, protesters opposed to the building of a new runway at the UK's Heathrow Airport formed a giant NO on the nearby fields.

Carbon offset schemes

Efforts are being made to make air travel more sustainable. New aircraft are larger, quieter, and more fuel efficient. Carbon offset schemes have been developed too. They allow air passengers to give money to an energy-efficiency project to compensate for the carbon emissions of their flight. For example, their donations might help to supply low-energy lightbulbs in Central Asia or fuel-efficient stoves in Mexico. Some environmental campaigners oppose carbon offset schemes, arguing that once a person has taken a flight, the damage has been done. They say it is wrong to ask someone else to clean up after you. Others contend that if people are going to continue to fly, it is better that they do something to offset their carbon emissions than nothing at all.

These women in Ngong, Kenya, are taking part in a carbon offset scheme—they are making a fuel-efficient stove.

A high price for flying

The best way to lessen the impact of flying is to fly less. Higher fuel taxes might encourage this course of action. They would prevent budget airlines from offering bargain flights and might make travelers think twice about taking short flights between cities. Yet some people believe this would make flying affordable only for the rich. Others point out that the people with the highest incomes fly most, while the poorest rarely do. So perhaps this measure is not as unfair as it seems.

Despite all these efforts, a central problem remains. Currently, no sustainable alternative to aircraft fuel exists. Some environmental campaigners maintain that flying is therefore not sustainable. They suggest limiting aircraft capacity, cutting down on short-haul (short) flights, and improving public transportation by road and rail. There are more realistic ways of making these other forms of transportation sustainable.

SUSTAINABLE TECHNOLOGIES

The fuel-efficient Airbus

The giant Airbus 380 is the largest passenger airliner ever built. It can carry 555 passengers in three classes. However, it could transport 840 people if there were only one, standard class. The Airbus has high-efficiency engines. The company that designed it claims these burn less fuel than a small car when calculated on the basis of the number of passengers the aircraft carries and the distance traveled. Special silencers make the plane quieter: it produces half as much noise as other jumbo jets. The plane is also built from lightweight materials, including carbon fiber.

Observers at Mumbai Airport, India, watch a brand-new Airbus 380 coming in to land. By October 2008, there were nine of these giant aircraft in operation worldwide.

CHAPTER 3

On the Roads

People love their cars. Cars are a status symbol in both developed and developing countries. It is a common belief that having a car gives you greater freedom and allows you to be more independent.

Since World War II, there has been a massive increase in car use worldwide. Most of this increase has taken place in the developed world. People are traveling farther and more often. Since 1980, as countries such as India and China have experienced rapid economic development, driving has grown there too. The number of cars on Chinese roads rose dramatically from 1 million in 1990 to 22 million in 2006. There has been a huge increase in road freight too. In Europe, the transportation of goods by road grew by 45 percent between 1996 and 2006.

More cars, more problems

Motor vehicles have become the most popular means of transporting goods and people, yet the cars and trucks on our roads are not sustainable because they rely on fossil fuels. The vast majority of vehicles run on gas and diesel, both of which come from oil—which one day will run out.

FACE THE **FACTS**

This bar chart shows the number of passenger cars per 1,000 people in five countries.

Country	Cars per 1,000 people
China	18
Ethiopia	1
India	8
UK	457
US	461

Source: World Road Statistics 2008

The huge increase in traffic on the roads causes congestion. More roads are built to reduce the congestion—and the number of vehicles using the new roads rises. People waste time sitting in traffic jams, and the delays are costly to the economy. In 2003, Americans lost 3.7 billion hours and 2.3 billion gallons (8.7 billion liters) of fuel from traffic jams.

Road building has great environmental costs too. Large areas of land are devoted to roads, parking and out-of-town developments such as shopping centers. New roads wipe out vast swathes of countryside and forests. For example, in recent years the Brazilian government has been carrying out a road-building program in the Amazon. Roads are important to the economy because they allow people access to the forest's natural resources. However, road building destroys the forest, which is already dying back because of the effects of climate change.

PERSPECTIVE

Roads destroy forests

"Once you build a road into a pristine [unspoiled] forest, you start an inevitable process of illegal colonization [settlement], logging [tree felling], landclearing, and forest destruction."

William Laurance of the Smithsonian Tropical Research Institute in Panama, speaking about the road development program in the Amazon, 2001.

Roads snake through Bangkok, Thailand. The city suffers from continual traffic jams. Despite the construction of a light rail system in the early twenty-first century, traffic congestion remains a problem.

Smog hangs over this busy highway in Beijing, China. Owing to the high levels of air pollution, some people in Beijing wear a face mask to prevent toxic particles from reaching their lungs.

Traffic and pollution

In addition to damaging the environment, road traffic can seriously harm human health. An estimated 1.2 million people worldwide are killed in road accidents every year, 85 percent of them in developing countries. Pollution is another danger. Gas fumes contain dangerous chemicals such as carbon monoxide, lead, and hydrocarbons. Diesel fumes contain nitrogen dioxide, sulfur dioxide, and suspended particulate matter (SPM). In high quantities, lead can cause brain damage, while SPM can result in breathing problems, including asthma. Children are particularly at risk.

Noise pollution is another problem for people who live or work near busy roads. A European survey in 2007 showed that people living in urban areas considered road traffic the most annoying form of noise pollution.

New car designs

Manufacturers are trying to make cars more environmentally sustainable. Cars are now constructed using lightweight materials, such as aluminum and plastics, because lighter cars require less fuel to power them. The design of engines, transmissions, and tires has been improved. Owing to such measures, fuel efficiency has gradually increased—by 8 percent between 1995 and 2005.

Yet vehicles could be made far more efficient if manufacturers accepted a decline in performance. Modern cars are extremely powerful. If they were designed for reduced acceleration and speed, they would use less fuel.

Cleaner fuels

Another area of improvement is the invention of cleaner fuels. In developed countries, lead is no longer used in fuel, and the amount of sulfur dioxide has been greatly reduced. However, in many developing countries, fuel still contains these pollutants.

To reduce or avoid the use of gas, hybrid and electric cars have been created. A hybrid car has an electric motor, powered by a battery, and a gas engine. The electric motor works while the car is traveling at low speed. The gas engine kicks in at higher speeds, when it operates more efficiently.

SUSTAINABLE TECHNOLOGIES

The Tesla Roadster: A special electric car

The Tesla Roadster is an electric sports car powered by a battery pack. It allows the motorist to drive for 217 miles (350 km) before recharging, and it produces no harmful emissions. The car's motor is very efficient, converting up to 95 percent of electrical energy into movement. The motor has just one moving part, whereas a normal car has more than a hundred, so the car is much lighter. The main drawback is the vehicle's price: $130,000!

Arnold Schwarzenegger, the governor of California, inspects a Tesla Roadster during a visit to the 2006 Los Angeles Auto Show.

There are several hybrid cars on the market, but not all motorists are prepared to switch to a new kind of car. Instead, many people have opted to use biofuels in their existing cars. Biofuels are renewable fuels such as ethanol and biodiesel, which are made from crops, including corn, sugarcane, rapeseed, and palm oil. Worldwide, the production of ethanol doubled between 2000 and 2005.

The pros and cons of biofuels

Those in favor of using biofuels say they reduce reliance on fossil fuels, which means that they are more sustainable. While the burning of biofuels releases carbon dioxide, the plants cultivated to produce biofuels absorb carbon dioxide while they are growing. However, those who oppose the use of biofuels argue that energy is required to grow and process the crops. In addition, if crops such as corn are grown to provide fuel, the amount produced for food is reduced. For example, in Malaysia, forests traditionally used by indigenous people have been destroyed to make way for palm oil plantations. Opponents claim that biofuels are not a sustainable alternative.

In this factory in South Dakota, ethanol is produced to power vehicles. The increase in ethanol production has been driven by concerns over high oil prices and climate change, but it may itself not be sustainable.

Car sharing

While people discuss how cars should be fueled, the fact remains that vehicles are not sustainable for other reasons too. Not least, they require roads and parking lots, and create congestion. In Australia and in some countries in Europe, there are schemes to help people use cars more wisely. People can join carpools. They advertise if they need a ride or can offer a ride to another traveler. Or instead of owning a car, people borrow one when they need it. The car is parked locally and shared by people in the area.

To reduce the amount of traffic on the highways, some congested regions, such as California, have introduced high-occupancy vehicle (HOV) and high-occupancy toll (HOT) lanes. Vehicles carrying more than one passenger and vehicles paying a toll (fee) are allowed to use faster lanes.

Every evening the roads in Los Angeles are jammed with traffic as people return home from work.

FACE THE **FACTS**

In 2000, drivers in central London, UK, spent 50 percent of their travel time in lines. In 2003, a congestion charge was introduced, which meant that motorists entering central London had to pay a fee. By 2008, traffic in the congestion zone had declined by 21 percent. Accidents and pollution levels had also decreased, while cycling within the zone had increased by 43 percent.

Back on the buses

Although the various methods of sharing private cars are extremely useful, public transportation is more sustainable—simply because each bus, streetcar, or subway carries a far greater number of passengers.

Buses are the most widely used form of public transportation in the world. The routes are flexible, and the vehicles can run on all kinds of roads. In many developing countries, there are inter-city routes between major cities as well as local bus services for short trips.

Nevertheless, traffic congestion means that bus transportation is not always convenient in city centers. In Curitiba, Brazil, the Bus Rapid Transit system was created to solve this problem. Five main bus routes run from the residential areas into the city center, like spokes on a bicycle wheel. Special bus lanes allow

Passengers alight from a bus in Curitiba, Brazil, into a raised tubular bus stop. People get on and off the bus at the same time through extra-wide doors. This measure, along with the pre-purchase of tickets, means the bus only needs to stop for 15 to 19 seconds.

the buses to travel quickly. To save time, passengers buy a ticket at the bus stop before getting on the bus. About 80 percent of travelers use the bus to reach the city center. The result is that car use is dramatically reduced. The Curitiba system is a good model for other cities to follow.

Inter-city bus travel could be improved, too. In the UK, for example, such buses are unpopular because they are slow. They spend a long time crawling through city centers to reach the expressway. One idea is to build bus stations at expressway intersections so that buses do not go through city centers. Buses could deliver passengers to the stations. This would be a more effective way of transporting people for medium distances than private cars. The road network is already in place, so the environmental cost of implementing the scheme would be low.

Streetcar lines

In some cities, the return of the streetcar system has provided a convenient mode of mass transit. Several cities in France have built new streetcar lines. In Paris, for example, the new T3 streetcar line, which opened in 2006, carries 100,000 passengers a day—twice the number carried by the bus service it replaced. The streetcars travel faster too.

FACE THE **FACTS**

According to transportation expert Alan Storkey, at any one time the M25 expressway around London can accommodate about 11,600 cars, carrying about 18,500 passengers (assuming an average of 1.6 people per car). If those passengers traveled in buses, the expressway could accommodate 260,000 people!

CHAPTER 4

A Return to the Rails

Many countries have a railroad system dating to the nineteenth century. Some, such as the US and UK, have allowed their railroad networks to decline. In places where there has been investment in rail travel, it usually proves to be a sustainable alternative to driving and flying.

The decline of the railroads is one reason why people in the US are so dependent on cars. During the nineteenth century, a good railroad network was built, but in the 1920s, cars started to become popular. There was a decline in the number of passengers using the railroads. After World War II, the US government supported the development of highways and airports, but it provided no financial aid to the railroads. Between 1945 and 1964, non-commuter passenger travel decreased by an incredible 84 percent, as Americans rushed to buy their own vehicles.

It is not just passengers who have switched to the roads. In many European countries, for example, freight transport has transferred from railway to road. The total amount of freight in the (then) 15 countries of the European Union doubled between 1970 and 2000. Most of this increase was divided roughly between road and sea transport.

FACE THE **FACTS**

Even when added together, trains and buses produce far fewer emissions than cars.

Type of transportation	Emissions (grams CO^2 per passenger kilometer)*
Private car	135
Train	50
Bus	30

* 1g per passenger km = 0.06 ounces per passenger mile

Source: *T618 Traction Energy Metrics*, Roger Kemp, 2007

The proportion of freight carried by rail in those 15 countries declined from 21 percent in 1970 to just 8.1 percent in 2000.

Bringing freight back on track

The switch to transporting freight by road is not sustainable for the environment and is worsening the problems of congestion and pollution. But this trend can be reversed. Trains have huge capacity, which means they are an excellent way to transport large quantities of goods. India has one of the largest and busiest rail networks in the world. Indian Railways runs about 5,000 freight trains a week and plans to increase freight by a massive 45 percent by 2011-12. If more goods are carried by rail, carbon emissions, and road traffic will be reduced.

India has an extensive freight train service. In addition, train cars carrying fruit and vegetables can be attached to passenger trains like this one. This increases the amount of freight that can be transported.

High-speed trains

It is also essential to encourage passengers to switch from cars and planes to trains. However, the service needs to be reliable, fast, and cheap for travellers to change their habits.

Some countries have invested in high-speed trains that travel at more than 186 miles per hour (300 km per hour). The Shanghai Maglev hurtles along at a super-fast 270 mph (430 kph). In Japan, the Shinkansen "bullet train" cruises at a slightly more leisurely 160 mph (260 kph). The Japanese government has invested in a network of high-speed railway lines in an effort to limit the number of cars on the roads.

There are some disadvantages to these fast trains, though. The networks are costly to build, and the trains are less energy efficient than those that run at normal speeds of under 125 mph (200 kph). Transportation researcher Professor Roger Kemp, from Lancaster University in the UK, has shown that if you double the speed of a train but keep everything else the same, the energy it uses increases by four times. This means that high-speed trains are only really sustainable if they run on renewable fuels.

The Shinkansen train network on Japan's main island of Honshu connects Tokyo with most of the island's other major cities.

PERSPECTIVE

Slowing down

"The Japanese have really tried to reduce energy and make their trains environmentally friendly. They go fast, but not super-fast... Progress is seen as carrying more people faster. But if we are going to seriously get back to anything that resembles carbon neutrality... we need to travel more slowly."

Roger Kemp explains how limiting the speed of super-fast trains is important for the environment.

Cheap and comfortable

It is possible to encourage people to use trains traveling at normal speeds. To begin with, rail ticket prices need to be competitive with airfares. Currently, rail travelers pay more the farther they go, so long journeys are usually more expensive by train than by air. Also, it is often necessary to buy a separate ticket for each leg of the journey, so booking a trip can be complicated. Bringing down prices could increase demand. Trains would be fuller and so more fuel efficient and more profitable to run.

Going underground

Rail transportation within cities can also be organized to reduce people's car use. In large cities, subways can provide a fast, efficient mode of transportation. Subways are more environmentally sustainable than cars. They are less polluting and reduce the problems of parking and congestion.

Moscow's underground stations are noted for their impressive architecture. In 2007-08, work began on expanding the ornately designed subway network even more to meet growing demand from passengers.

Several countries have improved their underground services. Moscow, in Russia, is a city of 10 million people. It has an extensive subway system that carries up to 9 million passengers every day. The trains are fast and frequent, the fares are low, and the stations are elegant too.

The subway in Dubai under construction. The trains offer compartments for women and children and a first-class section for business travelers.

Dubai, the largest city in the United Arab Emirates, has the most vehicles per person in the world. The Dubai subway opened in 2009 and is designed to provide a desperately needed public transportation system. It is expected to carry 355 million passengers a year.

Light railways

Underground systems like Dubai's are suitable for big cities, but for smaller or less wealthy cities, light railways are cheaper to build. These aboveground railways are built either on tracks on existing roads or elevated above the ground. They are similar to streetcar systems (see page 23). There are light railways in both developed and developing countries. They cross some of the mega-cities of Asia, including Kuala Lumpur in Malaysia.

In 1999, an 18-mile-long (29 km) light railway was built to reduce traffic gridlock in Kuala Lumpur. It runs from the east to the west of the city, through some of the most heavily populated areas. Fully automated and driverless, it provides a reliable service 18 hours a day. During peak hours, there is a train every 90 seconds! The network is linked to the city's bus and rail services.

Light railways have even become popular in car-dependent North America. In 2008, there were 21 modern light railways, with more planned. In Dallas, Texas, the Dallas Area Rapid Transit (DART) system opened in 1996 and has proved extremely successful. The number of passengers rose from 1.4 million in 1996 to 17.5 million in 2005. In addition to reducing car use, light railways can help to regenerate city centers by making it easier for people to travel in and out. After the DART system opened, new shopping areas and facilities grew up around the busiest stations of the network.

Provided that the type of development is tailored to the size and budget of the country or region involved, there are clear benefits to improving rail travel.

SUSTAINABLE TECHNOLOGIES

Light railway technology

In Angers, France, the light railway system is powered not by overhead wires but by a third rail positioned between the tracks. Power is supplied to the rail by underground boxes positioned every 72 feet (22 metres). It is sent to the segment of rail only when the tram passes over it. This makes the roads on which the tracks are situated entirely safe for other users.

In addition to a light railway system, Kuala Lumpur has a monorail (a railway with one track), which transports passengers around the main hotel and shopping districts of the city.

CHAPTER 5

Across Rivers and Seas

Water transportation ranges from small sailing boats to enormous oil tankers and cruise ships. Some boats offer a sustainable way of traveling, while others involve heavy fuel use.

Water transportation is crucial for international freight. Non-perishable goods (produce that can spend a long time in transit without spoiling) are often transported by ship. Of all forms of transportation, cargo vessels can carry the biggest loads—more than the largest aircraft—and they are far less polluting than air transportation. A study of the clothing industry in 2007 found that the greenhouse gas emissions produced by air freighting clothes were between 20 and 150 times greater than the emissions produced by sea freighting.

Send it by sea

Improved methods for transporting perishable goods are making sea freight even more environmentally friendly. The Israeli producer Agrexco has greatly reduced its use of air freight for fresh produce, from 88,000 tons (80,000 metric tonnes) in 2000 to about 27 to

FACE THE **FACTS**

This chart shows how far some fresh foods travelled to reach a supermarket in Toronto in 2003.

Food	Point of origin	Distance traveled miles
Swiss chard	Texas (via Los Angeles)	4,998
Pears	Portugal (via Halifax)	3,879
Apples	Washington (via Los Angeles)	3,658
Tomatoes	Pelee Island, Canada	224
Lamb chops	New Zealand	8,625

* 1 mile = 1.6 km

Source: Fighting Global Warming at the Farmer's Market, Foodshare.net, 2005

33,000 tons (25 to 30,000 metric tonnes) in 2007. Its new vessels have 18 different chambers, each with sophisticated temperature and humidity controls that are adapted to suit the goods being transported. Many shipping companies have taken measures to increase energy efficiency. Some have started to sail their ships more slowly, which is the best way to reduce fuel consumption.

PERSPECTIVE

Food miles

"In my own area, my food co-op sells organic apples from Washington State right next to apples grown locally and they both cost about the same. Locally produced, seasonal foods cut energy use and therefore leave a smaller impact. They are much, much better for the environment and for local economies."

Joshua Rosenthal, director of the Institute for Integrative Nutrition, New York City, 2008.

Eat local food

As individuals, we can try to reduce the need for long-distance transport. For example, people in developed countries are used to the luxury of buying foods from around the world. We can buy kiwi fruits from New Zealand or avocados from Mexico at any time of year. Consuming more locally produced goods can help to reduce "food miles". In the US, for instance, nearly all the wheat that is eaten is grown in the Midwest. In the early 2000s, farmers in different areas of the country, such as New Mexico, Massachusetts, and Pennsylvania, began growing wheat on small farms to supply local customers.

A farmers' market in Spain. Customers can buy food directly from local farmers, and they know that the produce is fresh.

Inland waterways

For moving goods short distances within a country and across the sea, the use of inland waterways could be increased. This type of transportation is safe, quiet, and energy efficient: one cargo barge can carry the same amount as 110 trucks! But if more boats are to use the waterways, it is important that river habitats are respected. Boat safety is vital to avoid accidents and the resulting pollution, which could damage the environment.

Passenger ships

Cargo ships are definitely more sustainable than air freight, but passenger travel by ship is more complicated. First, there is the issue of speed. As with the railroads, water transportation is more sustainable if the vessels move slowly. Freight is carried at relatively slow speeds, but passengers are usually in a hurry to arrive. Passenger ships cruise at about 34 mph (54 kph) which is far too slow for long journeys, for example, across the Atlantic.

Second, existing ships have high carbon emissions. It is estimated that a car ferry traveling from the UK to Norway produces carbon emissions about 20 times greater than those of a train traveling at 125 mph (200 kph), and even several times greater than those of a plane! A major problem is the weight of the ship, which carries a large number of vehicles. A ferry that carries passengers alone would be lighter and more fuel efficient, although the journey would still be slow.

Nevertheless, there are efforts to make passenger ferries more sustainable. In 2008, the H-ferry, a 100-passenger hydrogen boat, was under development in Amsterdam, Holland. The ferry has zero emissions. The energy to produce the hydrogen usually comes from burning natural gas, which produces lower carbon emissions than diesel. To reduce the emissions to zero, the makers of the H-ferry plan to use wind power to make the hydrogen fuel.

A passenger travels on a small ferry between the Swedish mainland and islands. A ferry service is essential for countries with many islands.

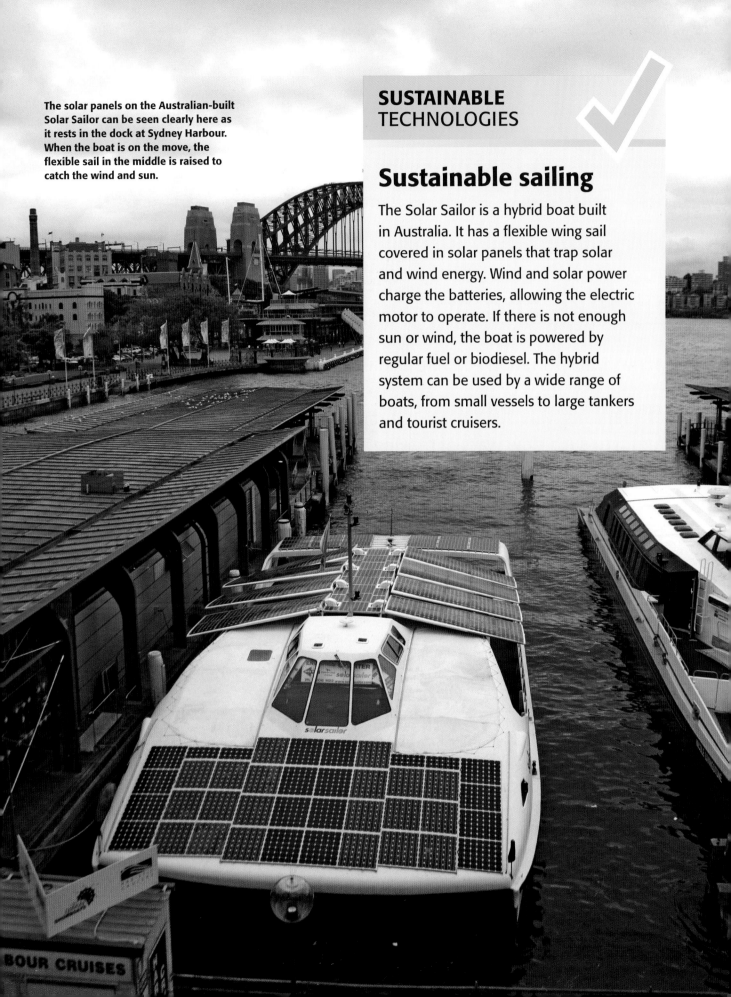

The solar panels on the Australian-built Solar Sailor can be seen clearly here as it rests in the dock at Sydney Harbour. When the boat is on the move, the flexible sail in the middle is raised to catch the wind and sun.

Sustainable sailing

The Solar Sailor is a hybrid boat built in Australia. It has a flexible wing sail covered in solar panels that trap solar and wind energy. Wind and solar power charge the batteries, allowing the electric motor to operate. If there is not enough sun or wind, the boat is powered by regular fuel or biodiesel. The hybrid system can be used by a wide range of boats, from small vessels to large tankers and tourist cruisers.

BOUR CRUISES

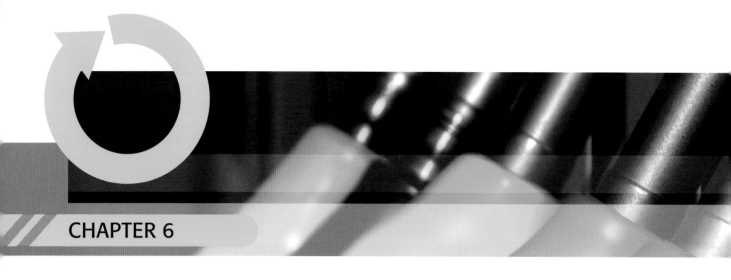

CHAPTER 6

By Bike and on Foot

Active transportation—cycling and walking—is the most sustainable form of transit, and the cheapest. In an age of super-fast vehicles, how can people be persuaded to return to such slow ways of moving around?

Bicycles as a form of transportation date to the early nineteenth century. In parts of the world where there are relatively few cars, bicycles are vital for transporting goods and people. Worldwide, there are twice as many bicycles as cars. Bikes are relatively cheap to buy, are easy to use, and require little maintenance. Cycling keeps people fit and active, too; it is a popular sport and recreation.

Healthy but unpopular?

Despite the benefits, in some Western countries, including the US, Australia, Canada, and the UK, it is hard to persuade people to leave their cars at home and cycle instead. In the rapidly developing countries of China and India, bicycle use has declined as increasing numbers of wealthier people have started buying cars. Cycling and walking are seen as low-status options—the ways that poorer people travel. People believe that driving is quicker, although this may not be true in congested city centers. In fact, cycling can be the quickest way to travel!

FACE THE **FACTS**

In 2008, the UK *Top Gear* TV show organized a race to see which form of transportation was quickest for crossing London from west to east in the morning rush hour. The four competitors used a bike, public transportation, a speedboat, and a massive Mercedes car. The cyclist won the race.

The benefits of walking are similar to those of cycling: it improves health and saves money. Walking is, of course, only suitable for short journeys. Yet many motorists drive even for these journeys. In Scotland, for instance, a 2005-06 travel survey showed that half of all car trips were of 2.5 miles (4 km) or less. For many of these trips, people could have walked instead. The car culture has affected people's health—those who drive everywhere often do not exercise enough. In developed countries, there is a crisis of obesity (people who are extremely overweight). In Australia, 17 percent of the population is obese. Returning to walking or cycling for short trips is not only more sustainable, it can also help people keep their weight down.

Cyclists and walkers take advantage of a car-free route through a park in Tokyo, Japan.

Walking buses

Although people may understand the benefits of leaving the car at home, they are unlikely to switch to walking or cycling unless these options are made more attractive. In countries such as the UK and Ireland, "walking bus" schemes have been established to encourage children to walk to school. These schemes offer social as well as environmental and health benefits. The children walk to school as a group, accompanied by some parents. There are "bus stops" to pick up children who live along the route. The walking bus offers an opportunity for fresh air, exercise, and a chat while reducing traffic around the school.

Children and parents going to school on a "walking bus" in London, UK. They wear fluorescent vests so they are easily visible to motorists.

Park and ride

Park-and-ride schemes are another traffic reduction measure. In many European and North American cities, motorists park on the outskirts and take a bus or train into town. This limits the number of cars entering the city center. Walking and cycling are much more enjoyable once the dangers and noise of traffic have been reduced.

Better by bike

In northern European countries, including Denmark, Germany, and Holland, policies were introduced in the mid-1970s to improve facilities for cyclists and pedestrians. Japan has also succeeded in encouraging active transportation.

In cities where the issues of safety and bicycle parking have been addressed, cycling has increased significantly. In Denmark's capital, Copenhagen, dedicated bicycle lanes were introduced in 1983 to protect cyclists from road traffic and pedestrians from bicycles. A curb on either side of the lane separates it from the road and the pavement. Secure bicycle parking is provided at stations and on the street (12 bikes can be parked in the space that one car requires!). In some cities, such as Paris, France, you do not even need your own bike. You can hire one from a rack in the city and return it to another rack when you have completed your journey.

PERSPECTIVE

On two wheels

"It's simply cheaper with your bike... With a car, you can't reliably predict how long your commute will be, but you can with a bike. You are not affected by traffic jams—you can just ride through them. It's a real advantage."

Cyclist Michael Abraham, Berlin, Germany, speaking in August 2008.

Cycling is not practical for everyone. Some elderly or disabled people may not be able to use a bike. Cycle rickshaws can help—these are taxis pulled by cyclists. They are found around the world, especially in Asian countries such as Vietnam, Cambodia, and India.

SUSTAINABLE TECHNOLOGIES

The e-bike

There are two types of e-bike. A power-on-demand bike allows the rider to pedal the bike but to switch on the power if he or she becomes tired. It can travel for 30 to 50 miles (50 to 80 km) before the battery needs recharging. A power-assisted bike does about half of the cyclist's work the whole time. E-bikes have a top speed of about 25 mph (40 kph). The legal limit in the US is 20 mph (32 kph). That's the same as the average speed of world-record-breaking cyclist Lance Armstrong over two hours! The cost of fueling an e-bike is a fraction of that of running a car. The energy used by a 100-watt electric lightbulb burning for an evening would be enough to power an e-bike for up to 40 miles (65 km).

This solar-powered e-bike can be pedaled or used with an electric motor. The motor is powered by electricity produced by the rectangular solar panel mounted on the front of the bicycle.

There are easy ways to resolve other issues, too. Although cycling can be unpleasant in the rain, wearing good-quality wet-weather clothing can help keep a cyclist dry. Sometimes cyclists need to carry luggage or passengers. Bicycle manufacturers have introduced covered trailers that can be attached to bikes for transporting cargo or small children.

E-bicycles

In areas that are just too hilly for cycling, or if commuters need to cover long distances, an electric bicycle, or e-bike, can help. This is a normal bicycle with a motor attached (see box).

Taking bikes for a ride

What about cyclists who need to travel between cities? The answer is to integrate cycling with public transportation. In Germany, for example, cyclists can take their bikes on the train. Most regional trains have special compartments for bikes—although it is not possible to take bikes on some long-distance routes. For this reason, folding bikes are becoming increasingly popular in both developed and developing countries. Light and compact, some of these bikes can be folded in just 15 seconds.

It is important to encourage people to use bikes as a method of transportation in developed countries. But it is also crucial to

These women in Burkina Faso use bicycles to transport themselves and their children, and bring home food from the local market.

promote the use of bikes in developing countries, both to stop the increase in cars and to provide much-needed transportion. In southern Africa, for example, there are schemes that import unwanted bikes from Europe, the Americas, and Asia. These are distributed to students so they can attend school and to health-care workers so they can visit their patients.

39

CHAPTER 7

A Sustainable Future?

In the future, new technologies will be developed to make transportation more sustainable. Yet many useful technologies already exist. A large part of the solution lies in creating an integrated transportation system and changing people's attitudes to how they travel.

Governments devise transportation policy. They have the power to increase funding for public transportation and to make it cheaper while reducing spending on road building. Local government authorities can reorganize road lanes to give priority to public transportation.

Paying the price

Pricing can also be used to encourage people to change their habits. Motorists who use particularly polluting forms of transportation can be asked to pay higher road taxes to reflect the cost to the environment. In the UK, a law in 2008 introduced higher taxes for "gas guzzlers" which are cars that emit large quantities of carbon dioxide, including 4x4s and sports cars. Cars that produce very low emissions, such as the Citroën C1, were rewarded with a special reduced rate of tax.

Higher costs do persuade people to make different choices. When oil prices rose steeply in

FACE THE **FACTS**

Internet technology can reduce the need to travel. Some people are able to work from home, accessing their office computer system. Instead of going to a meeting, they may hold a video conference. People can also shop online. Rather than traveling to the stores, they have goods delivered to their home. In this way, one delivery vehicle can replace many individual journeys.

2008, motorists in the US began to choose more fuel-efficient car models and cut down on non-essential trips.

Carbon rationing

Environmental campaigners have suggested introducing carbon rationing to reduce the world's carbon dioxide emissions. The agreed on figure for the amount of emissions that the world could emit would be divided by the number of people in the world. This would give each person's individual carbon ration. To work out a country's carbon ration, you would multiply this figure by the number of people in the country.

According to a simple system devised by Mayer Hillman and David Fleming, carbon rationing could be made to apply only to fuel and electricity. If everyone was given the same allocation, they could use it when paying fuel bills or buying vehicle fuel. Opponents of the idea say it would lead to a loss of personal freedom. They argue that travel options would be reduced. If flights were included in the ration, one return flight might use up a whole year's allowance.

Working from home: a boy living in the Australian outback, where there are no schools, communicates with his teachers via a two-way radio system.

Also, the poorest people often have the oldest and least efficient cars and cannot afford to buy a new fuel-efficient model. But supporters of carbon rationing say it is a fair system because everyone receives the same ration. People can buy or sell part of their ration according to their means. The wealthy Ferrari driver could buy extra rations from car-less bus users.

In 2007, protesters organized a climate camp in the village of Sipson, near Heathrow Airport, outside London. They demonstrated against the damage the airport causes to the environment.

Integrated transport

Another way of reducing emissions is to integrate transportation methods. Containerization has already improved the transportation of freight. It means that freight is loaded into a standard container that can be transferred easily between trucks, ships, and trains. In the US and some European countries, such as Italy, Germany, and Austria, RoadRailers are used. These vehicles can travel on roads and railroad tracks. In addition to improving integration, it is crucial to reduce the need for long-distance transportation by encouraging people to buy locally produced goods.

Public transportation needs to be well integrated too. In many countries, a lot of travel time is spent waiting for a bus or train to arrive. Rail, bus, ferry, and subway services can be coordinated to make travel more convenient. In Geneva, Switzerland, for example, the Transports Publics Genevois (TPG) operates most of the public transportation network.

PERSPECTIVE

Planning sustainable communities

"A change in land use planning is integral to ultimately solving our transportation problems. People want to live in sustainable communities where they can walk, bike, or take transit to work or school. Let's create them."

Ben Polley, Green Party of Ontario, Canada, speaking in September 2007.

There is a single fare system, which means you can buy one ticket for any type of transportation in the area. You can even buy a ticket to cover all your transportation for the year!

Changing attitudes

Even if public transportation improves, the challenge is to get people to give up driving and flying. This is the case both in developed countries, where people take their right to drive and fly for granted, and in developing countries, where people aspire to the same lifestyle as those in wealthier lands. In the end, avoiding the use of unsustainable transportation will mean sharing transportation with other people. It could be a pleasant, comfortable, and more sociable solution to our transportation problems.

These young people have opted to use the sustainable train for their travels. While flying often involves a lengthy wait at the airport and a trip into the city on arrival, the train usually takes passengers directly to the city center.

GLOSSARY

active transportation Walking or cycling.

automated Using machines and computers to do a job.

barge A large boat with a flat bottom, used for carrying goods and people on rivers and canals.

biodiesel A fuel made from vegetable oil or animal fat that can be used in a diesel engine, for example, in trucks.

biofuel A fuel made from plants grown for the purpose, as opposed to fossil fuels such as coal and oil.

carbon offset The giving of money to a project to help reduce carbon dioxide emissions; the offset is made to make up for emissions that a person has caused, for example, by traveling on a plane.

carbon rationing Giving everyone a ration that allows him or her to use a fixed amount of fuel.

climate change The long-term changes to the climate. These occur naturally but are occurring more rapidly because human activities are polluting the atmosphere.

commuter A person who travels into a city each day to work.

congestion A buildup of traffic caused by too many vehicles on the road at any one time.

congestion charge A fee charged to motorists when they drive through a congested area.

containerization The packaging of goods into standard-sized containers that can be easily transferred between different forms of transportation.

e-bicycle A bicycle with an electric motor to help the rider pedal it.

emissions Polluting waste products, such as carbon dioxide, that are released into the atmosphere.

ethanol A form of alcohol that can be used as fuel.

food miles The number of miles it takes for a food to travel from the place where it is produced to the place where it is eaten.

fossil fuel A fuel such as coal or oil, which was formed over millions of years from the remains of animals or plants.

freight Goods that are transported by ships, planes, trains, or trucks. Freight is also known as cargo.

fuel efficiency The efficiency with which a vehicle converts fuel into useful energy—a vehicle that uses less fuel is said to be fuel efficient.

hybrid A vehicle that uses more than one type of power.

indigenous people The people who originally come from a particular place.

Industrial Revolution The period in the eighteenth and nineteenth centuries in Europe and the US when machines began to be used to do work and industry grew rapidly.

internal combustion engine The type of engine in most cars that produces power by burning gasoline.

light railway A modern electric railway built in cities, usually running on its own lines but sometimes using roads.

Maglev A train that uses special tracks and that is propelled along by magnetic attraction between the train and the rails. It "floats" over the rails.

noise pollution A high level of noise that is unpleasant or harmful.

organic Produced without using manufactured chemicals.

regenerate To bring new economic growth to an area; this often involves improving transportation links.

renewable fuel A fuel that can be replaced naturally

and can be used without the risk of exhausting its supply.

solar panels Panels on a roof that collect energy from sunlight to heat water or produce electricity.

stratosphere The layer of the atmosphere between approximately 6 and 11 miles (10 and 18 km) above the surface of the earth.

streetcar A vehicle powered by electricity that runs on rails along the streets and carries passengers. It is often seen as a form of light rail.

subway An underground railroad.

sustainable Involving the use of products and energy in a way that does not harm people or the environment now or in the future.

transit The process of being moved from one place to another.

walking bus A group of children and parents who walk to school together.

waterway A river or canal along which boats can travel.

BOOKS

Bowden, Rob. *Sustainable World: Transport* Wayland, 2003.

Bowden, Rob. *Transportation: Our Impact on the Planet* Wayland, 2004.

Graham, Ian. *Machines at Work: On the Rails* QED Publishing, 2008.

Morris, Mark. *Cutting Edge Transportation: High Speed, Power and Performance* Heinemann, 2005.

Williams, Brian. *Transportation Technology* Smart Apple Media, 2008.

Williams, Harriet. *Road and Rail Transportation* Facts On File Inc., 2004.

WEBSITES

http://www.airportwatch.org.uk/
The site for AirportWatch, a UK group of environmental organizations that oppose unsustainable airport expansion.

http://news.bbc.co.uk/1/hi/sci/tech/6294133.stm
The *BBC Quick Guide: Biofuels* outlines the advantages and disadvantages of biofuels.

http://ec.europa.eu/publications/booklets/move/39/en.pdf
"Europe at a Crossroads: the Need for Sustainable Transport" is a European Union report about making transportation more sustainable.

http://www.geocities.com/sustrannet/actionguide/Outline.htm
A community action guide to people-centered, equitable, and sustainable urban transportation.

http://www.railway-technology.com/
A site about the railroad industry worldwide.

INDEX

Page numbers in **BOLD** refer to illustrations.